GET READY, GET SET, STAY PUT

Aging at Home and Other Options for Senior Living

By Emily M. Butler-Morton

Printed in the United States of America.

TABLE OF CONTENTS

Get Ready, Get Set, Stay Put

INTRODUCTION

"Setting a goal is not the main thing. It is deciding how you will go about achieving it and staying with that plan."

Tom Landry

Home. Comfort. Familiarity. Security. Nothing compares to kicking your shoes off, getting into comfortable clothing, walking into your own kitchen, grabbing a snack, and retiring to your own favorite spot, all in a secure familiar setting. Our home is our personal refuge, where we can enjoy just being ourselves, with our own rules, or no rules. It's a place where we can do nothing or something, with no time constraints. This is particularly true if we are in our retirement years. We need our home, that" centering place" to get refreshed, restored and renewed.

These things being said, you have probably selected this book because you are beginning to think about where, and how you might want to live, as you move into your senior years. You probably hope that you can age in place, right in your own home. Included in this book are the many possible ways to remain independent, live at home and enjoy your familiar surroundings well into your later years. Step by step measures are outlined on how to make your current home more safe, secure, and a place that meets your wishes and requirements. As we know from experience, good plans and best outcomes begin with a thorough and complete look at the existing situation. So the first goal is to do an honest assessment of your current circumstances.

Begin to Get Ready, Get Set, Stay Put!

CHAPTER ONE

GET READY

"Honesty is the first chapter of the book of wisdom."
-Thomas Jefferson

The Elephant

First, get rid of the elephant. You know that invisible entity looming in the room that no one wants to acknowledge. The first step is being honest with yourself about the elephant's existence. So you have a "talk" with yourself, and other parties, if appropriate. The question to consider is - realistically, will it be feasible for you to age in your own home, or do you need to make plans for other options? A viewpoint other than your own can be helpful. You might find that you will be able to be more objective if you include a trusted family member or friend in the conversation.

The main issue is whether or not you are still safe in your own home. For instance, have you been taking some falls, or forgetting to take your medicine? Are things piling up around the house that you don't feel like taking care of? Are you very lonely or depressed? Is preparing a meal too much of an effort for you? Is your pet being properly cared for? How about outside-is your yard in need of cleanup or removal of unused items? Or, maybe you are just tired of home ownership responsibilities!

THE ASSESSMENT

Is it possible to make your home senior friendly by making some changes and doing minor alterations to provide a safe and secure environment? What are your medical issues? How much can you afford?

Remember this: It is never too soon to start, but it might be too late to begin, if you put it off. Don't be caught in that nightmare situation where you have to make a rapid haphazard decision. Or, worse yet, have someone else make the decision for you because you are unable to.

So, let's get to the assessment!

Begin by looking at the three most import areas of the assessment phase.

1. SAFETY

2. MEDICAL

3. FUNDS

<u>Safety</u>

1. Where will you be the safest? Is it possible that your current home can be made "senior safe?"
2. Does your home have stairs?
3. Is the home overcrowded with extra furnishings, making it easy to trip or fall?
4. Is the current home in a neighborhood or in an isolated area?
5. Who will look in on you if you stay in your own home? For those living alone and aging at home, there

are various agencies who will check in on residents on a daily basis, such as the R.U.O.K., a program run and operated by volunteers, under an umbrella organization. The volunteers make a daily call to registered seniors to see if they are okay.

6. There are also many medical alert companies and check-in systems available for purchase in most communities, as well. Some of these alert systems can have a medication reminder feature included.

Medical

1. Record information on any special medical issues. Some medical issues will require specific living accommodations.

2. What arrangements have been, or will be, made for getting to and from medical appointments?

3. Are there medical specialists readily available in the future or present location?

4. Will there be a hospital close by?

5. Are new Medicare patients accepted by the Doctors in the desired location?

6. Do you have access to someone who can take medical notes when you go to the Doctor? Amidst all the confusion and medical jargon, it is helpful to have someone else who can listen and record.

7. Do you have a long term care policy, and when and how can it be used? Each insurance company is different and you will need to check with the insurance representative to see what is covered.

Funds

1. Explore current expenses and outgo. This may seem tedious but it will pay off in the long run. Write down actual expenditures-total for month and year. Do a cost comparison of monthly expenditures of proposed costs of moving to a community or remaining in your own home.

2. Determine which assets, if any, can be converted to cash. Can the house be sold and the money put into an interest-bearing account? Can a car be sold when it is not needed?

3. Possibly through downsizing and selling of items, extra cash can be accumulated and placed in a savings account.

4. Do you pay for unnecessary services and subscriptions-magazines or online accounts?

What to do next?

Chapter Two will include important documents to have in place, appropriate steps to take, and will help you to Get Set for the best possible "unique-to-you" living set-up.

CHAPTER TWO

GET SET

"If I had eight hours to chop down a tree, I'd spend six sharpening my axe."

— Abraham Lincoln

Being prepared ahead of time is key to any successful endeavor. Too often we wait until the last minute and experience the "deer in the headlights" scenario. Suddenly we must do something—and we are not prepared, so we just do *something!*

Being honest and open with yourself and/or loved ones about future years will definitely have its benefits and will result in the best possible outcome.

As you continue to work your plan, the following are some fine-tuning ideas that will best prepare you for your goal.

Paper Trail

Ensure that you have a "paper trail." This can be a simple binder with a page for information containing important contact information. For instance, there should be a page with all the pertinent information on you and other important people in your life. This would be everything from date of birth, birthplace, medications, allergies, children's names, physician's contact information, etc. Addresses of banks and financial institutions should be included. Names of pets, the veterinarian, and pet medical records can also be considered. There should be information on burial plans, wills and testaments, etc. As you can imagine, the more information included in this document, the easier it would be for someone to step in at time of crisis. Include anything important to you in this document.

The "paper trail" should provide a thorough source of information that could be easily accessed at a time of emergency.

Advanced Directive

An Advanced Directive is a legal directive that allows you to make your family aware of your medical/healthcare wishes. In the event of something happening to you, i.e., stroke, coma, or any other situation that would prevent you from expressing yourself, this document will take the stress off of family members having to make the decisions for you.

An Advance Directive is also identified as a Durable Power of Attorney for Healthcare. Both of these forms can be obtained online, from hospitals, from your physician, or from an attorney.

The Will

A Will makes clear who will receive your assets and personal property. A Will helps to avoid disagreements over your estate, after your death. There are many types of Wills. It is best to seek the counsel of an attorney to discuss what would work best for you.

Burial Plans

While discussing funeral and burial plans may be awkward and uncomfortable, it is wise to make these decisions in advance as a way to ensure that your needs and wishes are respected. Having these things in place will also relieve family of the burden of decision-making during a difficult time.

Downsizing

Another way to prepare for the future is to begin to lighten the load. Maybe it's time to begin downsizing. Even if a move is not imminent, simplifying and getting rid of clutter can make a living space more "livable" and safe.

A TRIED AND TRUE DOWNSIZING METHOD:

Go to an area or location where none of your "stuff" is in view. One thing that works well is to make a list. The only way to be objective during this process is to go to a room or location where you cannot see all of your stuff. Take a piece of paper, draw a line down the middle. On one side put NEEDS and on the other WANTS. This takes some thought because we often think our wants are our needs. A good way to look at needs is "what do I actually use on a daily basis?" (It can be a surprisingly few things.)

NEEDS	*WANTS*
Dresser	Wicker Loveseat
Bed	Antique Book Collection
Sofa	Grandfather Clock
End Tables	
T.V.	

This may take a few tries, but it seems to bring clarity to the decision. You will probably find that your "needs" column may be larger than your "wants" column. The secret is to keep as many of your "needs" with you and only a few of your "wants." If a person is just not ready to dispose of, give away, or sell a lot of things, renting space in a local storage unit is helpful. This allows for time to decide what really fits into the new home. It is also a good way to see what you can live with or without.

<u>TRUE downsizing story</u>

Mom had lived in her home for 47 years. Dad had passed away recently. With my busy career and other family responsibilities, it had not been possible for me to spend more than a couple of hours a week with her. (Consequently, she was feeling lonely and isolated.) She and I had explored the possibility of her staying in her home and decided we would work towards that goal. Then she could enjoy her familiar surroundings, friends, and church close-by, and keep the same doctors, etc. The challenge was to scale down to make everything mom needed more manageable.

Together, Mom and I came up with a plan. First, to be objective, we took a pen and paper and went to a location where all of the stuff was not visible. We then drew a line down the center of the paper - on one side put "NEEDS" and on the other side put "WANTS." It was surprising how short the list was on the "NEEDS" side of the paper. We found that the "WANTS" side was a little longer and had to work on it a couple of times. What Mom ended up doing was giving some of her favorite pieces to family members, knowing that she could "visit" her stuff on occasion. She also stored some things in a local storage unit for later review and consideration. The rest was given to a local charity. That way there were no hurried goodbyes to any of Mom's stuff. This lessened the impact of a major lifestyle change and made my mom's home more safe. - Contributed by S. Benson, San Diego, Ca.

Estate Sales

If you are planning to stay in your own home, an estate sale can be beneficial in that it is a great way to downsize, clean out the extra stuff, and make a little extra money.

In some cases, an Estate Sale Professional can be hired and is the answer to effectively scaling down. Or, you may want to have your own sale.

If moving to another location, all furnishings and items can be left in the house and priced for sale. An event such as this is usually held over a 1-2 day period. For anyone who wants to start over, buy new furniture and other household furnishings, or just "lighten the load", this is a great option.

Once you've done your footwork and paperwork, you will have a good assessment of what "stuff" you will actually need for a comfortable lifestyle. This can be a "freeing" event. It is amazing what we can live without!

Now that you have finalized your paperwork and downsized some of your belongings, you are in position to work on your "Staying Put" plan. Chapter Three is full of options to help you create a safe and comfortable situation and at the same time retain your independence.

CHAPTER THREE

STAY PUT

Your word is a lamp to my feet and a light to my path.

-Psalm 119:105 NIV

Staying Put

There are various housing options for individuals as they age. Living in your own home where you are familiar with everything is a preferred choice. Where a person chooses to live, as they age, is a major factor in determining a person's level of contentment. A person's own home represents security and independence, and most people would rather just stay put in their familiar surroundings as they grow older. While this may be the desired outcome, it is important to understand that in some cases this will not be the safest and best solution for all elderly persons.

If you are able, and want to stay in your own home, there are many ways to make a home safe and comfortable. We will go through the most important living areas with some general thoughts about the overall home, as well.

Bathroom

- Grab bars
- Walk-in shower or tub/shower combination
- Non-slip surfaces in tub
- Phone in bathroom
- Night light
- High-boy toilet
- Hot water temperature set to prevent scalding
- Free Standing sink for wheelchair access
- Motion Detector Light in Bathroom area

Bedroom

- Sturdy bedside table
- Lamp easy to reach/turn off and on
- Clear path between bed and bathroom
- Rugs have non-slip backing
- Comfortable chair for rest or when dressing

Kitchen

- Dishwasher at waist height
- Can frequently used items be reached without a stool
- Fire extinguisher within easy reach
- Work area where person can sit when preparing food
- Is work area efficient—considered layout
- Drawers and cabinets should have D shaped handles
- Counter tops at convenient height
- Appliances with side by side doors

There are builders and handymen who cater specifically to senior/elders. They specialize in safe environments. You can usually find one in the yellow pages under builders. Part of the ad will say something like "senior safe remodels." If you do not have someone in your family who can do repairs and remodel, this is a good option.

Other Thoughts About Overall Home and Amenities

- Security System installed
- Handrails securely fastened
- All areas well lit
- Rocker light switches to turn lights off and on from different locations.
- Electrical outlets should be higher on the wall than the code says and there should be many
- Is a telephone accessible at all times in all locations?
  Are smoke detectors installed and batteries replaced on a regular basis?
- Clutter?
  Emergency buttons or "lifeline"
  (Some Police Departments offer cell
  seniors which are programmed with telephone
  number of their local Police Department)

- Cupboards and under-cabinets should have as many sliding drawers as possible for easy access and less lifting. When possible, door knobs and faucets should be lever type.
- Garage- hang a tennis ball from ceiling to hit car windshield when parked at right spot.
- Doggie/cat door-area where pet can go out safely.
- Washer/dryer close to where most laundry is generated.
- No throw rugs
- Re-think flooring; does it have to be vacuumed or washed frequently?
- Paved driveways/walkways
- Doorways at least 36 inches wide for wheelchair/walker access.

OTHER OPTIONS FOR AGING AT HOME

As an alternative to remodeling your home, there are other options on how to stay "at home" and live independently. Here are a few.

Move in with family

Some families have "granny flats", or small apartments on their property, where aging loved ones can live, yet still maintain a sense of independency and have their privacy.

In times of need, there is always someone close by and if the family takes a vacation or is away for a time, there is still a presence on the property.

Rent from Adult Children

After owning their own home (s) over a span of 55 years, it seemed difficult for Mr. & Mrs. J. to think of renting from their son. But through no fault of their own, and due to a downturn in the economy, it became necessary to make some creative choices. Moving into a beautiful patio-home in a lovely neighborhood in McMinnville, Oregon, has turned out to be a blessing in disguise for both parents and son. Purchased as an investment by their son, Mr. & Mrs. J., are enjoying a beautiful home in a lovely neighborhood, paying a very modest monthly rental rate. They still enjoy complete independence and privacy, have some of the responsibilities of home ownership, but are freed up from major repairs or paying property taxes, etc. Their son puts monthly rental payments into an interest bearing account. The accumulated funds are there to be used at some point in time should a move become necessary for Mr. & Mrs. J. to move to some type of senior living community. This is a "win-win" for both sides of the family, and an investment in the future no matter how you look at it.

House sharing

Sharing your home or apartment with friends might be a viable solution for anyone wishing to remain in their own home. It can provide elderly homeowners with added income as well as security and companionship. This could be set up similar to a college roommate situation where each individual has their own private space, i.e. bedroom and bathroom with common areas being shared by all.

College or Nursing Students

Sometimes if carefully researched, you can let a room to a nursing student from a local college or any student who is looking for a secure atmosphere in which to study, sleep and eat. Extreme caution must be used here. References should be required.

CHAPTER FOUR

REMAIN INDEPENDENT ON A LIMITED BUDGET

The best way to have a good idea is to have a lot of ideas.

-Linus Pauling

This chapter covers possible ways to live a quality lifestyle on a fixed income. There are many services. My list is a sampling of what is available nationwide. Your local Agency on Aging is another good source to learn about local options.

HOUSING

Resources for Low Income Elderly

For most elderly poor, housing represents the number one expense. For the poor and economically vulnerable, the cost of providing and maintaining shelter will consume a third or more of total income. Many elderly folks spend their "golden years" living at the poverty level. There are some helps for these situations.

Subsidized Housing

Most States offer varying levels and varieties of subsidized housing for senior citizens in the lower income brackets. A good place to start when looking into special housing options for the elderly is American Association of Homes and Services for the Aging (AAHSA).

One of the more popular programs is through HUD Supportive Housing for the Elderly Program (Section 202), which provides low income elderly with options that allow them to live independently but in an environment that provides services such as cleaning, cooking, transportation, etc. Section 202 is available to low income households comprised of one member at least 62 years of age at the time of occupancy. More information about this program can be obtained by going to HUD Multifamily Housing - Program Description at **hud.gov**

For additional information about subsidized housing go to: **huduser.org**

Many of the non-profit senior living organizations offer subsidized low income housing to the elderly population. Another good website for information on low income housing for most States is **lowincomehousing.us**.

While there are various offerings of non-profit senior communities, it should be noted that having non-profit status does not guarantee lower rates. Careful research must be done. These homes can be researched online by searching for non-profit or not-for-profit senior living or retirement for the State you are interested in.

FOOD/MEALS

Jewish Family Services JFS provides kosher meals on wheels to eligible seniors in some communities. Go to **jewishfamilyservice.org** for information nationwide.

Volunteers of America Meals on Wheels or Food for Friends

Nutritious home-delivered meals for homebound older adults 60 years of age or older who live in many counties. No one is denied service due to an inability to contribute toward the cost of the meals. Seniors receive daily hot meals or frozen meals for the coming week.

More than 50% of the seniors receiving this service will rely on this delivery as their one and only complete daily meal. Additionally, the seniors receiving Meals on Wheels are often isolated and their daily visit from the Meals on Wheels volunteer may constitute their only daily human contact. Seniors regularly experience an improvement in physical well-being and have an enhanced ability and willingness to remain in their own home as a result of these program services.

Food Bank Locator**:** To find food banks throughout the U.S., go to the following website.

feedingamerica.org/foodbank-results.aspx.

Supplemental Nutrition Assistance Program (SNAP). This is a nutrition service/program offered to low income citizens nationwide. Access this organization on U.S. Department of Agriculture at **usa.gov**.

OTHER SERVICES

There are various member-driven nonprofit organizations across the country that will provide services such as transportation, home repairs, social activities, errand running, and other helpful services that seniors may find hard to do on their own. These are run by volunteers and limited paid staff.

One of these is the Village to Village Network (VTV), based in St. Louis, Mo., with communities nationwide. **vtv@network.org.** Various independent residential communities across the nation have joined forces with VTV to enhance their amenity package. It is a wonderful alternative for anyone in need of a little help in order to continue living independently in their own home.

Aging Together (**agingtogether.org**), an agency in Virginia, serves seniors by forming partnerships with area professionals to provide education, hosts guest speakers, and keeps the community aware of available services and events.

It goes without saying, most people would prefer to stay in their own home and enjoy what they have been accustomed to, but at some point if this is not possible, a move to some type of senior living community will be required. This will be determined once all resources have been explored with the primary concerns of safety, medical requirements and funding being taken into consideration. If you do find yourself in this category, the next couple of chapters provide information on the various types of senior communities and what might be best for you.

CHAPTER FIVE

SENIOR LIVING COMMUNITY OPTIONS

The remarkable thing is, we have a choice every day regarding the attitude we will embrace for that day.

-Charles R. Swindoll

Certain issues indicate that a move into some type of senior living or retirement community would be best. The following is a list of possible signs that an elderly person would be more appropriately cared for in a senior community.

INDICATORS

Following is a list of signs and indicators that a person may not be safe living alone.

- Poor and Declining Health
- Inability to bathe, groom, walk, take medications
- Frequent falls

- Prolonged depression
- Housebound
- Chronic pain
- Substance abuse
- Unsafe home atmosphere
- Loss of appetite
- Loneliness
- Loss on interest in cleanliness

This is only a partial list and it is important to involve the physician in a move to a senior community. (See Chapter Seven-How to Determine Levels of Care for more information.)

TYPES OF SENIOR COMMUNITIES

Following is a discussion of the different types of senior-living communities. This will help you to make the best choice for yourself or a loved one. If you are the adult child and are doing this for a parent, this will probably be one of the most difficult things you will ever do. Making the choice for yourself will be a little less difficult.

Independent Living

An Independent Living Community is designed for people who can, and are able to, live independently but do not want to maintain a home with all of the home ownership responsibilities. In an Independent Living Community, you will most likely find people of the same age and interests. Most Independent Living communities offer activities and prepared meals along with a large array of amenities. There will be stimulating activities, educational trips, craft and painting classes, swimming, exercise, and much more. The move to a good independent community can be a fairly smooth transition offering a lifestyle similar to living at home, with some very nice added advantages —no meals to cook, no yard work and little or no housecleaning. More often than not, the new resident is amazed at how much the new lifestyle offers them more freedom, fewer worries, and new opportunities.

Assisted Living

Assisted living is for people needing assistance with Activities of Daily Living (ADLs), but wish to live as independently as possible for as long as possible. Assisted living serves as a bridge between independent living and nursing homes. ADLs such as eating, bathing, dressing, laundry, housekeeping, and assistance with medications are provided. Prior to moving into an Assisted Living Community, a prospective resident is assessed and an appropriate level of care is determined. Some communities include the first level of care in the monthly rental amount. Residents are usually re-assessed on an ongoing basis to ensure that proper care is being given. Often residents improve and a lower level of care can be administered, creating more independence for the resident and lowering the cost, too. There should be a detailed daily plan for your loved one. This is a document that the staff is required to follow and fulfill. You are entitled to a copy of it.

Assisted Living is not an alternative to nursing or memory care. However, some Assisted Living Communities do have memory care units for those suffering from Alzheimer's/dementia.

It should be noted that extra caution should be taken when considering an Assisted Living Community. There will be various levels of care offered. Each additional level of care will incur added cost. You will want to have a detailed copy of the Levels of Care rates before you sign a contract. Sometimes an individual starts out a higher level of care and after settling in, will need less assistance, thereby reducing the care needed. This should be closely monitored by family members or a physician to assure appropriate care level is being administered.

Skilled Nursing Facilities (SNF)

Skilled Nursing Facilities (SNF) and Nursing Homes are designed to care for very frail people who are not able to care for themselves and have numerous health care requirements. People in SNFs and Nursing Homes are pretty much bed-bound and have an inability to ambulate on their own. Some nursing homes have memory care units where people with Alzheimer's and dementia can live comfortably.

Admission to a skilled nursing is administered by the Physician.

Alzheimer's/ Memory Care/ Dementia

Some Skilled Nursing Communities have Memory Care Units where people with varying degrees of memory loss can be accommodated.
There are some Assisted Living Communities that work very well for people with dementia, depending upon the level of dementia. This can be determined by the staff and the resident's physician.

A good Alzheimer's Unit is designed in a certain way for good reason. For instance, the floor should be simple, without complicated designs. Confusion takes place if there is too much variation in the floor coverings and the patient may be afraid to take a step. Shadows are confusing too. The lighting should be bright but not glaring. Noise level should be low to avoid agitation caused by loud noises. Residents' rooms should have identifiers such as large decals or a certain color to aid the resident in finding his room. Entryways should be alarmed and locked in a true Alzheimer's unit. Hallways should all lead back to the same place to prevent the patient from getting lost. There should be plenty of space to walk. Staff should be available for residents who tend to wander at night or for those who have Sundowner's Disease (Rupp, Joyce 1999).

Before admitting anyone to a dementia/Alzheimer's/ memory care unit, the physician must be consulted and a physician's report or History and Physical (H&P) is required by the admitting facility. Sometimes a psychological evaluation must be included in the admitting paperwork.

Six-Packs

An Adult Foster Care is basically the same as a Board and Care Community. These communities are small, usually found in a large home within a residential neighborhood. They typically have six bedrooms and have been nicknamed "six-packs." These are ideal for people who want a small, intimate, family-type atmosphere. Meals are served at a family style table where all residents eat together. There is usually a living room and TV room where residents gather. Many of these communities have a nurse on staff or on-call. The residents can enjoy activities and private transportation is provided for trips to the doctor and shopping. Legitimate Foster Care homes are licensed by the State and have strict regulations. Unlicensed homes do exist but are not recommended.

Continuing Care Communities (CCRC)

CCRCs combine independent living, assisted living and nursing care, and sometimes a memory care unit. Upon entrance to a CCRC you typically pay a large down-payment with sizeable monthly payments for your accommodations. When you buy into a CCRC you are assured that you will have care for the rest of your life. The downside is that in many of the CCRCs you can only receive a portion of your investment back should you decide that the community is not right for you. The bottom line is this—the longer you live in a CCRC, the less of your investment you will receive back, and at some point, determined by the particular community, none of your investment will be returned. Carefully review the contract before signing.

This option is the first choice of some folks wanting the security of knowing, that no matter what, they can live in the chosen community for the rest of their life. In other words, if you become seriously ill, you will not have to relocate. This may vary with different communities, so, read the fine print. It is also worth noting that a prospective resident must go through rigorous testing to be accepted into this type of community. An individual is required to have near perfect physical, mental, and psychosocial health.

Rental Communities

There are various types of rental communities for seniors. In some, you are required to pay an entrance fee and make a commitment to a long-term lease. Others are on a month-to-month basis with a 30-day notice to vacate requirement. The attractive thing about a rental situation is that you are free to invest your money elsewhere, and if the community doesn't suit you, it is easy to move to a new location.

Many of the senior living rental apartments are very small, have minimal services, and fewer amenities. They are often subsidized by the county or government. But for those on a limited budget this is an excellent option. Due to their popularity there is typically a long waiting list. It best to get on the waiting list well in advance of when you will need to move.

Independent Buy-in Communities

This is a special category that is often overlooked when researching senior living options. In this setting, residents buy their home or condo and are free to sell to anyone within the age requirement listed in the bylaws. These communities usually do not look like a retirement community, rather more like an upscale neighborhood with manicured lawns and yards. A clubhouse, dining room, and sometimes a putting green and pool are included. This type of neighborhood is particularly adaptable to the "Village" type umbrella program. See Chapter Four (**vtvn@network.org**

Moving to any type of senior living community represents a major life transition and should be approached cautiously.

It is important to ask a lot of questions, look at everything cursively before making a decision. Knowing the right questions to ask, what to look for, and what to actually do before signing a contract is of utmost importance. Too often folks do not receive the services that are promised prior to move-in. This can be avoided by asking the right questions, looking everything over carefully, and doing thorough research. Once the move is made, it is very difficult to make another move. A good resource to guide you is, "Care Enough to Know-Keep Your Parents Safe", by Emily M. Butler-Morton. The book includes an all-inclusive list of over 100 questions and items to be explored prior to making a move.

Chapter Six includes some additional ideas to look at while doing your planning and research

CHAPTER SIX

OTHER HELPS

Make sure you have a "Plan B." In other words, link up with others who can help out with your parents if you are not available. This will be especially important for long distance care giving. Enlist family members or friends who live closer to your parents to help out when you cannot be there. Perhaps there is a next-door neighbor who would be willing to help out at times.

Involving Siblings in Eldercare

It is common for one or two adult children in a family to manage the entire task of caring for their aging parents. Whether this is due to proximity, scheduling, expertise or just a sense of responsibility, it seems to be the norm. Not only can this lead to burnout, but may create resentment and family arguments.

Unless you are an only child or the lone relative of an aging loved one, there is always the

possibility of someone else helping with the care. Sometimes out of a sense of duty it is "easier" to do it all yourself. So, the first thing to do is ask others if they would like to be involved in the care. If others in the family decide to take on some of the care it is important to see who will do what and when. Consider each person's schedule. Also consider each person's strengths and weaknesses. Remember to discuss role reversal and what that might mean. An excellent book covering role reversal is "Caring for your Aging Parents, by Barbara Deane, Nav Press, 1989.

Use modern technology. Inquire about tele-medicine health monitoring systems where a patient can connect with a physician through an on-screen system where they can be diagnosed. Consider medication reminder systems where the patient receives a call when it is time to take meds.

Invest in pill dispensers, lifeline or other medical alert systems, and large-number telephones.

Do your parents have the tools they need to make life easier? This could be something small like an automatic can opener, a grabber to reach things in high places, and a large button universal remote.

There are hundreds of devices available online and in medical device stores.

Contact the agencies close to your parents' home to ensure that they have all of the services they are entitled to. Meal programs, care programs, and many social services are available through individual counties and are there for the asking. Churches and other community groups enjoy reaching out to the elderly too.

Consider a good in-home care service. This will take some research. These agencies can provide assistance with cooking, cleaning, transportation, grocery shopping, grooming as well as companionship. It is a good idea to talk to others who are familiar with the in-home care services in the area. Some agencies are better than others. Always ask the right questions before hiring a care giving agency. Ask for references, talk to others who have used the agency. Interview individual caregivers before they serve your loved ones.

Stay in touch and know what is going on. Do this by connecting with everyone and anyone in your parents' life, such as neighbors, a pastor, friends, or anyone that sees them more often than you are able to. If possible, give them a cell phone with important numbers programmed in.
Include numbers of the doctor, church, special friends, and of course, your number. Don't be surprised if you get a lot of calls at first.

Geriatric Care Manager

A geriatric care manager can be a special help if it is hard for you to get away. Geriatric Care Managers can initiate, coordinate, and launch a complete care program for your elderly loved ones - all in your absence. They will even arrange for ongoing care. The cost varies depending upon the area, in most cases between $70-$200 per hour is standard. Lump sum contracts are also available for specific situations such as research and preparing a Medicaid application.

To stay mindful of how your loved ones are doing it is a good idea to compare notes with others who are familiar with them. Sometimes when we are absorbed in a situation it is possible for our emotional involvement to shade reality.

GIVING UP THE DRIVER'S LICENSE

Ouch! What does the driver's license represent to most people? The first thought that comes to my mind is "independence." Relinquishing this precious privilege may trigger strong emotions causing anger, sadness, depression, a feeling of "giving up", or resentment toward the individual who initiated the decision.

There are some suggestions that will tend to ease the situation somewhat. Invite the driver to evaluate his/her own driving skills.

The following issues need to be considered:

- Ability to see clearly after dusk or dark
- Difficulty in reading road signs?

- Difficulty hearing?
- Tendency to get lost?
- Fear of traveling side by side with large vehicles
- Slow reflexes
- Have difficulty parking
- Difficulty turning head due to arthritis or other condition?

If the case where an accurate self-evaluation is not possible, and a senior appears to be an at-risk driver, the doctor can make an anonymous report to their state's Department of Motor Vehicles.

These laws vary by state but usually the DMV can often revoke driver's licenses in this way.

Sometimes this is the best solution, relieving the family from making the decision and becoming the group "who made me give up the keys."

In any event, discussing this issue with seniors requires sensitivity to their feelings. You can also help ease the blow by being prepared to suggest alternatives—such as taxis, mass transit,
senior-center shuttles, or other community transportation for seniors.

Attention Caregivers!

If you are caring for a parent or elderly loved one, you are a key person in knowing their needs. Caregivers frequently experience burnout and, subsequently, failing health from the constant draw on their emotional, mental, and physical health. Not only do your loved ones or friends have needs, but you do too. If you have been, or are currently the caregiver, your needs may dictate a change in living arrangements for your loved ones. You may have immediate family responsibilities and a career, in addition to your caregiving duties, often described as the "sandwich generation." It is important to encourage your loved ones to be as independent as possible. This will help you and them. Most adult children and/or caregivers have no healthcare training and can be bogged down by the demands of loved ones who are unable to take care of themselves. (Hutchinson, Joyce, Rupp 1999).

CHAPTER SEVEN

HOW LEVELS OF CARE ARE DETERMINED

Following is a typical evaluation tool used to determine the appropriate level of care when considering Independent Living, Assisted Living or Nursing Care. Each community will differ somewhat on determination of cost and what is included in each level.

MOBILITY*

Moves about independently. Able to seek and follow directions. Able to evacuate building independently in case of emergency. **(1 point)**

Ambulates with cane or walker. Moves about independently with wheelchair but needs help in case of emergency. **(2 points)**

Requires occasional assistance to move about, but usually independent. **(3 points)**

Mobile but requires assistance in moving about due to confusion, limited vision or weakness. **(4 points)**
Assist in transfer to and from bed, chair or toilet. **(5 points)**

Requires transfer and transport assistance. Requires turning in bed and in wheelchair. Probably needs a Skilled Nursing Facility. **(6 points)**

* The rule of thumb for Assisted Living Communities is that the resident must be able to stand, pivot, and transfer with little, or no assistance.

NUTRITION

Able to prepare own meals, eats without assistance. **(1 point)**

Can do some meal preparation, but needs main meal prepared daily **(3 points)**

Needs all meals. **(4 points)**

Needs assistance with eating, opening cartons, cutting food. **(5 points)**

Needs reminders to eat and assistance when eating. Probably needs a Skilled Nursing Facility. **(6 points**)

<u>HYGIENE</u>

Independent in all care including bathing, shaving, dressing. **(1 point)**

Assistance with hygiene. **(3 Points)**

Dependent upon others for all personal hygiene. **(6 points)**

HOUSEKEEPING

Independent in performing housekeeping functions including bed making, vacuuming, cleaning, and laundry. **(1 point)**

May need assistance with heavy housekeeping, vacuuming, laundry, changing linen **2 points)**

Needs laundry and housekeeping services provided. **(4 points)**

DRESSING

Independent and dresses appropriately.

(1 point)

Requires assistance with shoelaces, zippers, medical appliances or garments, or may require reminders. **(4 points)**

Dependent upon others for dressing. **(5 points)**

TOILETING

Independent and completely continent. (**1 point)**

Incontinence, colostomy or catheter but is independent in self-care. **(2 points)**

Occasional problems with incontinence, colostomy or catheter-care. **(4 points)**

Cannot manage incontinence or may require physical assistance with toileting on a regular basis. **(5 points**)

Regularly and uncontrollable incontinence or unable to communicate needs**. (6 points)**

MEDICATION**

Responsible for self-administration of medications. **(1 point)**

Able to self-administer medications, but needs reminders and monitoring of process**. (3 points)**

Family or home health agency administers medications. **(4 points)**

Cannot administer own medications. Medications must be administered by licensed professional. **(6 points**
** States Regulations vary regarding administration and storage of medications. It is necessary to check the state regulations for the community being considered.

MENTAL STATUS

Oriented to person, place and time. Memory intact with occasional forgetfulness with no pattern of memory loss. Able to reason, plan, and organize daily events. Can identify environmental needs and meet those needs. **(1 point)**

Orientation to person, place and time may be minimally impaired. Requires occasional direction or guidance when getting from place to place. May have occasional confusion causing anxiety, withdrawal, or depression. **(3 points)**

Poor judgment. May require strong orientation assistance and reminders. **(5 points)**

Disoriented to time, place and person, or memory is severely impaired. Unable to follow directions. Probably needs a memory care facility. **(6 points)**

BEHAVIORAL STATUS

Copes well with inner stress, deals appropriately with emotions and deals appropriately with others **(1 point)**

Periodic intervention from others to facilitate expression of emotions or periodic outbursts of anxiety or agitation. **(5 points)**

Maximum intervention is required to manage behavior. May cause danger to self or others or is abusive or extremely un-cooperative. **(6 points)**

INTERPRETATION

It is important to remember that all communities are different and have their own method of evaluating residents. On the following page you will find guidelines that will give you a general idea of appropriate placement for your loved one. There are gray areas and many times placement is open for interpretation by staff conducting the interview. should also be noted that a resident's scores may change on different days according to health status and medication. This needs to be discussed with the physician.

Now go through each section, add up the totals, and check against the following grid.

TOTAL: ___________

SCORES

34-50: Residents of Nursing Homes****

19-40: Residents of Assisted Living Facilities

13-23: Residents of Congregate Senior Housing Communities/ Supportive Housing

8-18: Residents of Independent Living Senior Apartments

***If a candidate scores a 6 in any category, probably the most appropriate level of care will probably be a specially equipped assisted living facility or a nursing home.

CHAPTER EIGHT

STAYING VITAL

Just like maintaining a vehicle, it takes continual attention and upkeep to keep your body in optimal running condition. When an automobile gets a certain number of miles on it, the tires need to be replaced. Our body is no different. There is ongoing care needed to ensure quality of life and vitality. In our retirement years we have more time to pay attention to these issues. This can be a time to restart your *engine* and refuel your energy level.

Being retired brings with it new considerations and adjustments. No matter what your age or how early or late you retire, it will be a major life-style change.

At first, retirement may mean no schedule, no daily/hourly obligations and plenty of freedom. You are your own boss. You can be alone or with people-your choice. You begin to do the many things that you could never get around to. You basically come and go as you please. There are many choices! Everything is pretty much centered around you, what you want to do, what makes you happy, what you want to buy, who you want to see.... This is fun for a time, in most circumstances, at some point, the newness wears off and a certain amount of emptiness may occur.

Maybe you miss the interaction on a daily basis with your co-workers. Maybe you yearn for the daily routine, maybe you are feeling un-useful or un-needed. Maybe you are without goals.

A good place to start is by taking a personal inventory, of sorts. How is your personal operating system or how about your hypothetical tires? On a vehicle, once the tires have been replaced, and the needed service performed, the car runs much more smoothly. It is the same with our body if we pay attention to what is needed and take measures to fix what is broken.

"Re-Tiring" in Retirement

Consider the following areas of your life. How is your ongoing maintenance and upkeep when it comes to diet, exercise, attitude and spirituality? Let's start with the diet.

DIET

Are you taking care to give your body the best fuel to function at its best? Sometimes quality far outweighs quantity – smaller amounts of wholesome food as opposed to junk food can make a difference in your overall feeling of wellness. Do you stay hydrated? Remember, our body is about 60% water, which needs to be replaced on a regular basis. No matter what the weather hot or cold, dry or wet, we need to drink plenty of fluids.

As in our car, when we put cheap gas in the tank we get less than good performance. We get sputtering, stopping, stalling, and no oomph! Once your diet is on the best track and you are powered up, you will have more energy. You will feel more like doing physical activities and exercise. Your "get up and go" button will be more responsive.

EXERCISE

So what are you doing to energize your body and build strength? A daily regimen for activities and exercise is ideal. But if you can only handle three days a week, that is fine. Simple walking can do wonders for your heart and your appearance. Breathing fresh air while exercising is advantageous as well as working out at a gym. If you have trouble with ambulation, chair exercises can be very helpful. Group exercises are fun but if you are not a part of a group there are videos for purchase or exercise programs on T.V. Always give your body time to adapt to any new exercise to avoid sore muscles and strain.

Along with good physical exertion, equally important is the way you face the day-how and what you think about things. Your attitude!

ATTITUDE

Attitudes can be changed. But it takes a decision of the Will to make it happen. It has been said that your heart will follow your head.

Is it time for an attitude adjustment? How do you see the world? Are you excited for the new day to begin? How do you see others in your life? Are you an encourager? Do you see the best in a situation, and in the people around you? Are you dwelling on the past - something you can do nothing about? Are you holding a grudge or harboring resentment? Do you judge yourself and people you know? Can you give constructive criticism? Can you take constructive criticism? It has been said that, "our attitude determines our altitude". Spend time with people who lift you up. Be one who lifts others up.

SPIRITUALITY

What is the source of your inner strength? Are you a praying person? Do you have a habit of meditation? Are you making quiet time for yourself to re-center? How do you calm yourself down? Do you have a support group of like-minded friends or family?

The above listed aspects of your life, diet, exercise, attitude and spirituality are areas that need continual attention. If you are one who doesn't already possess positive lifestyle habits, it is NEVER too late to start new. Feeling good about these important areas will give you new vitality creating a desire to want to do more. You will also sleep better and you will be a better friend, neighbor, mom, dad and/or spouse.

<u>Going Beyond Me, Myself, and I</u>

The whole goal of this chapter has been to consider how we can remain vital throughout our retirement years. If you have carefully considered the thoughts and suggestions presented on how to stay vital you are probably ready for some ideas on how to share this vitality with others. So, first let's see what you are good at, what your strengths are, and what you might like to do.

Reaching out can be the key to avoiding depression and sinking into that dark place of "woe is me." Getting out of yourself and reaching out to others can be a cure-all. Not only does it help someone else, it can make you feel better too.

Consider asking yourself the following questions to fine-tune a good fit for you. Discover how you can raise the gauge on your vitality meter by extending your reach and giving back.

1. Ponder your likes and dislikes
2. What are you good at?
3. What are you not so good at?
4. Are you a "people" person?
5. Are you a leader or a follower?
6. How much time do you have to give away?
7. Do you like to teach?
8. Which age group do you feel most comfortable with?
9. Do you like behind the scenes volunteer activities?
10. Do you do better in groups or with individuals?
11. How can you use your wisdom and knowledge to benefit others?

It is extremely important to remember that all vehicles and/or people are not created equally. Some are fast, some are slow, some are large or small. The important issue here is to use our personal vehicle for the purpose it was created for.

Following are some ideas on how you might use some of your talents and interests to boost the gauge on your vitality meter.

- Try a new class.
- Volunteer at the Library.
- Give a Mom a Day Out.
- Give a Caregiver a few hours off.
- Call someone that you are thinking of.
- Write a note to a friend.
- Smile at someone.
- Say hello to someone.
- Compliment someone.
- Listen to someone without being anxious to tell your own story.
- Offer to cook a meal for someone.
- Look for needs in your neighborhood that you can fill.
- Write a book.

- Try a new hobby-sell what you make at a craft fair.
- Learn to do something you thought you could not do.
- Teach a class.
- Volunteer at a community organization.
- Knit some hats to give away (if you are a knitter)
- Pick a flower and take it to a neighbor.
- Join a gardening group.
- Join a book discussion group.
- Spend a half hour just listening to someone else's problems.
- Give some of your stuff to someone who can use it.
- Teach Sunday School.
- Throw a "just because" party for some of your neighbors.
- Organize a neighborhood Bible study or prayer group.
- Start a walking group with neighbors.

Thinking and serving others is something that everyone can do in some form. The ideas are endless. Only you know what is the best way for you to reach out.

Are you interacting with others on a regular basis? Do you make opportunities to reach out with unconditional expectations? A trip to the grocery store and a simple smile given to a passerby goes a long way, both for the giver and receiver. If you can't go out, there is always the telephone. Do you know friends that would like to get a thoughtful note from you?

Remember, we don't have to be a victim of "aging." It happens to all of us.

It is like the little boy who was standing up in his high chair. His mom told him to sit down. He sat down, all right, but inside he was standing up! Despite our age or any maladies that might befall us, we can be victorious over them. Even if it is just making a thoughtful phone call, writing a note or smiling at someone and calling them by name. There are things we can do every day to give of ourselves and we will be better for it.

As Winston S. Churchill once said, "*We make a living by what we get. We make a life by what we give.*

ABOUT THE AUTHOR

Emily M. Butler-Morton, resident of Virginia, author, senior advocate, and public speaker. B.S. in Psychology/Family Studies and Certificate in Gerontology. Served for more than 25-years influencing, teaching, counseling, and guiding seniors and their families in matters related to senior living arrangements.

Following her career in Senior Living, Morton has continued her advocacy through lectures, community college classes, books, and seminars to serve and educate the elder population and their loved ones on how to effectively select the best and appropriate senior living lifestyle.

Get Ready, Get Set, Stay Put

26709437R00048

Made in the USA
Columbia, SC
17 September 2018